Easy Glass Etching

Easy Glass Etching

Marlis Cornett

Sterling Publishing Co., Inc.
New York

Prolific Impressions Production Staff:

Editor in Chief: Mickey Baskett

Creative Director: Joel Tressler

Graphics/Photography: Joel Tressler

Styling: Joel Tressler, Marlis Cornett

Administration: Jim Baskett

Library of Congress Cataloging-in-Publication Data

Cornett, Marlis.
    Easy glass etching / Marlis Cornett.
        p.   cm.
    Includes index.
    ISBN 1-4027-1406-8
        1. Glass etching--Patterns. I. Title.
    TT298.C67   2004
    748.6'3--dc22   2004009102

10 9 8 7 6 5 4 3 2 1

Published in paperback in 2006 by Sterling Publishing Co., Inc.
387 Park Avenue South, New York, N.Y. 10016
© 2004 by Prolific Impressions, Inc.
Produced by Prolific Impressions, Inc.
160 South Candler St., Decatur, GA 30030
Distributed in Canada by Sterling Publishing
c/o Canadian Manda Group, 165 Dufferin Street,
Toronto, Ontario, Canada M6K 3H6
Distributed in the United Kingdom by GMC Distribution Services,
Castle Place, 166 High Street, Lewes, East Sussex, England BN7 1XU
Distributed in Australia by Capricorn Link (Australia) Pty. Ltd.
P.O. Box 704, Windsor, NSW 2756 Australia
Printed in China
All rights reserved

Sterling ISBN-13: 978-1-4027-1406-1 Hardcover
        ISBN-10: 1-4027-1406-8

        ISBN-13: 978-1-4027-3461-8 Paperback
        ISBN-10: 1-4027-3461-1

For information about custom editions, special sales, premium and corporate purchases, please contact Sterling Special Sales Department at 800-805-5489 or specialsales@sterlingpub.com.

Acknowledgements

Thanks to Dremel Corporation for generously supplying the Diamond Tip Bits and Flex-Shaft used to create the projects in this book.

Dremel
4915 21st Street
Racine, WI 53406
www.dremel.com

CONTENTS

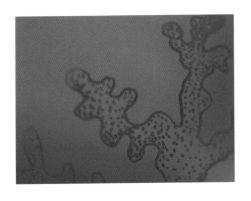  

About the Author

Marlis Cornett received her BA in Fine Arts from Kenyon College in Gambier, OH and went on to study illustration at Portfolio Center in Atlanta, GA. As an accomplished calligrapher and artist, Marlis is always experimenting with different mediums and has happily applied her skills to etching on glass. What began as a hobby has blossomed into another career path – her designs have quickly become in demand. In Easy Glass Etching, Marlis shares her secrets to successful glass etching.

Special thanks...

to Lynn for her expert editing advice.
to Brad for listening, advising, and providing unyielding support.

-M.C.

Etched glass accentuates any style of décor -- it can be everything from exquisitely sophisticated to fun and whimsical. Whatever style you choose, this book has plenty of ideas to get you started. *Easy Glass Etching* demonstrates simple techniques and provides step-by-step instructions accompanied by design patterns and color photos. Soon you will be on your way to creating personalized, etched glass masterpieces – most in less than 30 minutes!

This book is designed especially for beginners. Learning this exciting new craft is fun and easy by following our simple instructions. Various tips and techniques will lead you through each project. You can begin by using our project pattern designs. As you gain knowledge of the techniques, you can use this book as a launching pad for creating your own, unique and exciting etched glass projects.

All of the etching in this book is done with a small, inexpensive and easy to use hand-held electric rotary tool. Etched glass is permanent and actually carved into the glass; there are no messy or toxic chemicals involved. You will be amazed at the professional results you can achieve using the simple techniques we outline for you.

There are over 30 design projects with patterns, hints and tips to help you master the basic techniques of etching on glass. Projects are organized into five categories: Party Themes, Accents for the Home, Holidays, Gifts and, my favorite, Just for Kids and Pets. Several example projects include how to create a beautiful vase out of a recycled glass bottle, etch a personalized bowl for your pet, or create your own holiday ornaments. Each provides detailed step-by-step instruction and suggested techniques to create your own etched masterpiece.

You will soon be on your way to creating your own designs, the possibilities are endless – Enjoy!

BASIC TOOLS
AND
MATERIALS

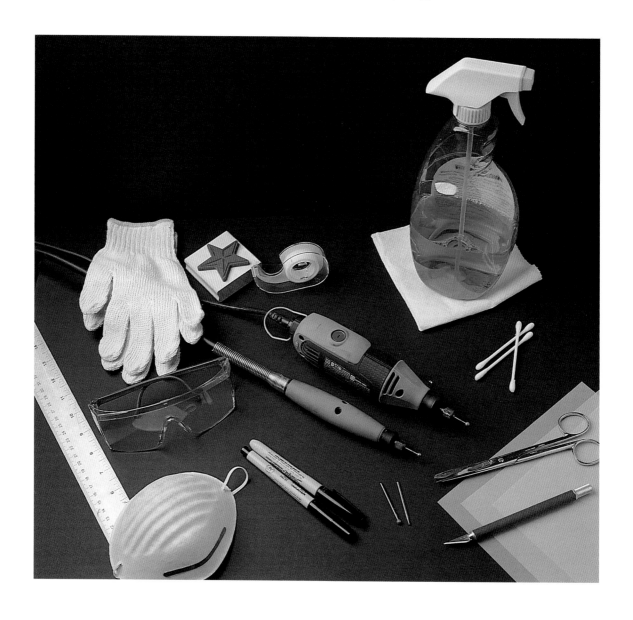

Hand-Held Electric Rotary Tool

There are several brands of hand-held rotary tools available at hardware stores, craft stores, and department stores. Whichever you choose, it is important to familiarize yourself with the manufacturer's instructions, guidelines and safety precautions for the model you select. The tool is relatively inexpensive and, with the proper attachments, can be used for many other tasks--anything from woodworking to filing your pet's nails.

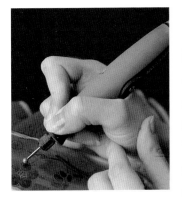

Flexible Shaft Attachment
(optional but highly recommended)

This is an attachment for the rotary tool that makes etching considerably easier -- much like the feel of writing with a fat permanent marker. The modest investment is well worth the price, especially when you're etching on a regular basis.

Diamond Point Bits

These are the only type of bits strong enough to etch the surface of glass. Diamond point bits have tiny diamond chips on the head of the bit. There are several sizes available. This book uses only two.

Glass

You will need an assortment of glass for practice and to use for the final projects. A wonderful source is the recycle bin. But remember - reserve your favorite shapes for finished projects. Glass is also relatively inexpensive to buy. Check your local discount stores. Also, keep your eyes open at garage sales. The grocery store can be a wonderful source for glass as well. I have often purchased a new variety of preserves based entirely on the container! Finally, a terrific source of glass is your local glass cutter. Not only can you have shapes custom cut, but also inquire about salvaging some scraps. I would be wary of taking any broken pieces, but you can tape the sharp edges with heavy masking tape. Glass is fragile, so always handle with care.

Permanent Markers

You will need a large marker and a fine tip marker. These are used to draw patterns on the glass to use as a guide. Although they are considered permanent, the markers will wash off the glass easily with soap and water or glass cleaner. However, before using a marker on any piece of glass, test a small area on the bottom and make sure that the ink can be removed.

Glass Cleaner, Paper Towels, Cotton Swabs

These are wonderful aids in cleaning off the ink marks and also correcting areas in the drawing.

Masking Tape

Tape is perfect for securing the design patterns onto the glass. Double-sided tape works nicely as well.

Safety Mask

It is a good idea to take precautions. Etching glass creates a soft powdery dust that may be harmful to breath.

Safety Goggles

It is important to protect your eyes from the dust created by etching the glass.

Cotton Gloves (optional)

These are wonderful to wear while etching the glass. As the pattern is etched, the white powder-like dust gathers around the design. With these soft gloves on, you can just brush away the dust with your hand as you work.

Carbon Paper or Transfer Paper

This can be used for transferring patterns. For example, a narrow bottle neck might prevent you from placing the pattern inside. You can use carbon paper to lightly transfer the design pattern directly onto the surface.

Dark Construction Paper/ Dark Colored Towel

By placing a dark piece of paper or poster board on your work surface, you will be able to see the etched areas more clearly. In some cases, a dark towel is useful for cradling a piece of glass that would otherwise roll on a hard surface.

Other Supplies

These items are useful aides for many of the projects, but not always required. Each project will include a list of essential supplies.

- Copier
- Light Box
- Scissors
- Spray adhesive
- Stylus
- Ball Point Pen
- Ruler
- Measuring Tape
- Craft Knife and Blades
- Tracing Paper

Before embarking on an exciting project, take a few minutes to set up your work space and familiarize yourself with the materials.

1. Set up a work area. It is important to choose a location that has good ventilation and adequate light. A comfortable work table and chair are important. Place a dark piece of paper onto your work area. Gather materials and arrange them within reach.

2. Choose some glass to use for practice. Remember, etching is permanent so choose a piece that you will not want to use in a future project. Clean the glass to remove any labels, dirt or dust. For practice, choose a form that has a flat surface. It will make it easier for you to get used to using the tool.

3. Lay the glass on the dark surface. If you only have round forms, use a dark towel to cradle the glass. *See photo 1.*

photo 1

4. After reading the manufacturer's instructions and safety guidelines carefully, fit your rotary tool with a diamond point bit.

5. Now it is time to play and experiment. Hold the tool as you would hold any writing utensil. *See Photo 2.* **Note: Low to medium speeds work best for etching glass.** Do not use the high speeds for our projects. Begin applying light pressure to the glass. Then apply moderate pressure. However, try not to apply excessive pressure; it will only cause the diamond point bit to wear out faster. After making a few marks, try drawing a few lines, polka dots, or squiggles onto the glass with the permanent marker. Then go back with the tool and trace the patterns.

photo 2

Low to medium speeds work best for etching glass. Do not use the high speeds for our projects.

6. Continue experimenting until you feel comfortable and familiar with the tool.

Once you feel comfortable using the hand-held rotary tool, it's time to choose a project. In this basic technique section you will find all the information required for creating and transferring patterns as well as instructions and techniques for etching the glass. To ensure quick, easy and beautiful results, it is important to take the time to read through the techniques that we refer to in each project. With our easy to follow instructions and guidelines, preparation is simple and etching becomes fun and easy.

Using Patterns

All of the projects in this book have design patterns included. Patterns are extremely easy to use, especially on clear glass projects.This section explains various ways to transfer our provided templates onto your desired piece of glass. We begin with the basic technique for transferring onto clear glass followed by easy techniques and tips for positioning the template designs. Then we move onto alternate techniques required for colored glass as well as odd shapes. You will find a variety of ways to use patterns, all of which are clearly outlined and designed to make your project as easy as possible. All of our patterns are printed to the actual size of the pictured projects. However, you can adjust the size of a pattern on a copier to fit your piece of glass.

Basic Techniques for Transferring

This is the easiest method and the most commonly used in this book.

1. Make a copy of the pattern using a copier or tracing paper to trace the pattern. Don't cut up your book to create a project! The patterns are printed to the actual size for our projects. If your glass piece does not match the dimensions of our project description, simply adjust the proportions of the design template by reducing or enlarging on a copier.

2. Place pattern inside or behind the glass and position in the desired location. A ruler is helpful in lining up the image. *See Photo 1*

photo 1

3. Secure the pattern with masking tape or double stick tape.

4. Although it is possible to begin etching and using the pattern as your guide, I have found that the surface of the glass can play tricks on your eyes. So, the best way to avoid this is by tracing the pattern with a marker on the surface of the glass. *See Photo 2*

photo 2

5. Fill in all the areas you want to etch with a black marker. If there is a lot of black in a design, go ahead and fill it all in, this way you will not etch any areas by mistake. Note: It's a good idea to make sure that your marker will wash off of each glass piece you use by testing a small area on the bottom.

6. Survey the traced pattern and make sure everything has been copied accurately before removing the tape and pattern. Glass cleaner and cotton swabs are useful if you need to erase any marks.

Setting up Guidelines

Some projects will ask you to set up guidelines to trace patterns. For example, when tracing a border or type font pattern onto glass, it is important to trace the design in an even line. To ensure that you do not get a slanted border, follow these easy steps.

photo 3

1. Using a ruler, measure down from the edge of the glass (see project instructions for exact measurements). Mark this measurement with a tick mark using the permanent marker. *See photo 3*

2. Repeat tick marks every 1-2 inches.

3. With the marker, connect the dots to form a line. This line represents the top of the border. Do the same for the bottom baseline of the border. You can also use a tape measure to connect the dots and trace a straight line. *See photo 4*

4. When transferring and etching the design, stay within these lines. *See photo 5*

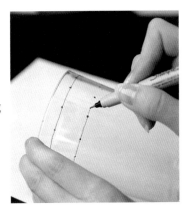

photo 4

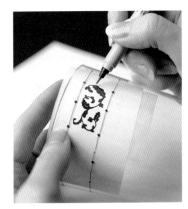

photo 5

Sizing and Transferring Repeat Borders

First determine the size of the pattern for your project and glass piece.

1. Place the pattern inside or behind the glass.

2. Use a permanent marker to dot the beginning and the end of the pattern on the glass.

3. Now move the pattern to the right so that the beginning of the border lines up with end of the last tick mark. Continue measuring all the way around the glass in this fashion. This is used to roughly estimate if the pattern will fit the entire circumference or length of the glass. You may need to increase or decrease the size of your pattern. If your pattern does not fit the circumference of your

glass, follow the instructions for determining enlargement percentage described in the next section.

4. Set up guidelines as explained in the previous section.

5. Trace your pattern inside of the guides with a marker. Work in sections until your pattern fits around the glass. If your pattern does not fit, you will need to reduce or enlarge on a copier as explained in Determining Enlargement Percentage.

Determining Enlargement Percentage

1. Measure the circumference of your glass (the distance around the outside of the glass where you plan to etch the pattern).

2. Measure the length of your pattern.

3. Divide the circumference by the length of your pattern. This equals A.

4. Take A and round it down to the nearest whole number. This equals B.

5. Divide A by B to get enlargement factor.

6. Multiply enlargement factor by 100 (move the decimal two spaces to the right) and you now have the percentage required.

> Example:
> 1. Your glass circumference is 10"
>
> 2. Your pattern length is 3"
>
> 3. 10 divided by 3 equals 3.33 (A)
>
> 4. 3.33 rounded down to the nearest whole number is 3 (B)
>
> 5. Divide 3.33 by 3 to get 1.11 (A/B - the enlargement factor)
>
> 6. Multiply 1.11 by 100 and you get 111%
>
> 7. Increase your pattern on a copier to 111% of original size.

Tracing Type Fonts

The easiest way to use a type font for a pattern is by typing in the letters, words, or phrases on the computer and then printing a hard copy. If a computer is not available or a type font style is not accessible, use our provided patterns to trace your letters. This will take a little more time, but works just as well. You will need tracing paper, ruler, pencil, eraser, marker, and light box. If a light box is not available, you can use a window in your house during daylight hours and tape the type font alphabet onto the window and then tape the tracing paper on top. *See photo 1.*

photo 1

1. First be sure the type font is the correct size for your project. You may need to use a copier to increase or decrease the size.

2. Tape the font alphabet on the light box.

3. Tape tracing paper over the alphabet.

4. Draw a line in pencil with the ruler. This will serve as a guideline for your word or words.

5. Use a pencil to trace the outline of the desired letters.

6. Go over the pencil with a dark marker.

7. Erase any extra pencil lines.

Alternative Transferring Techniques

Some glass forms make it difficult to transfer a pattern using the basic techniques. For example, a bottle with a long narrow neck prevents the insertion of a pattern. Or sometimes the glass may be a dark or opaque color or even filled with a candle! It is still possible to use the provided patterns. However, all of these circumstances make it necessary to use another transferring technique.

Transferring with Carbon Paper

1. Make sure the glass surface is clean and dry.

2. Place pattern face up directly on the area to be etched.

3. Secure with masking tape on two sides.

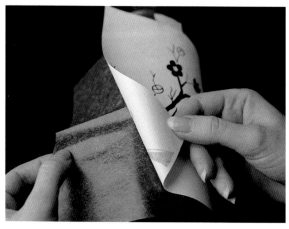

photo 2

4. Slide in the carbon paper, face down in between the glass and the pattern. *See photo 2.*

5. Use a stylus or ball point pen to trace the pattern.

6. Work in small sections and check to be sure that a mark is showing up on the glass. It will be faint but dark enough to use as a guide. The carbon tracing can easily rub off. So as you trace each section, go in with the permanent marker and darken the lines on the glass surface. Leave one side of the pattern taped so your design does not shift. *See photo 3.*

photo 3

photo 4

7. Do not remove the masking tape until you are sure that you have traced the entire pattern.

8. Be sure to fill in all areas you wish to etch.

Using Stencils

Stenciling is another easy method to transfer onto dark or opaque glass surfaces or pieces that do not allow a pattern to be placed inside. Stencils can be purchased in craft stores but you can also make your own using most of the project patterns.

1. Choose a pattern and resize on a copier if necessary.

2. Print or trace onto cardstock paper (80 lb. paper stock). Note: if you do not have access to a copier and wish to trace onto the cardstock, use a light box or tape the papers to a window and trace using carbon paper. *See photo 4.*

3. If you are making a stencil for a word, do not create a stencil for each letter; create one stencil for each word.

4. Once the image is on the paper, use a craft knife to cut out the dark areas of the pattern. *See photo 5.*

5. Now you have a customized stencil! Tape it in place on the glass and trace with a permanent marker. *See photo 6.*

photo 5

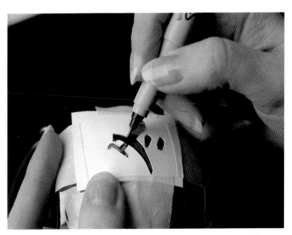

photo 6

Alternative Transferring Techniques

Using Rubber Stamps

This is an incredibly easy way to get a pattern onto any piece of glass, especially those that make tracing a difficult task. There are thousands of stamp designs available online and in craft stores. Although none of the patterns used in this book are rubber stamps, store bought stamps can be used as a substitute.

1. Make sure the glass surface is clean and dry.

2. Test the stamp ink on a small part of the glass to make sure that it can be removed. You can also apply acrylic paint onto the stamp and use this instead of ink. It will wash off if not left on for long periods of time.

3. Stamp the design in the desired location. *See photos 1 and 2.*

4. Allow ink or paint to dry.

photo 1

photo 2

Using the Computer

A computer can be very useful in preparing design patterns. It is wonderfully easy to choose a font and type out the names or phrases and print them to use as patterns. You can easily scale letters to the desired size and space. If you have a scanner for your computer, scan in the patterns and adjust size as necessary.

Be Creative

There are so many wonderful patterns included in this book, but don't forget that you can create your own designs easily. Use the marker to draw out polka dots, swirls or flowers and etch your own inspirations. Although this book is not designed for children, you can include them in the creative process by having them draw onto a glass plate and then an adult can etch their design for them. The possibilities are endless!

Look Around

Use this book as a launching pad. We have provided many patterns and ideas to get you started, but this is just the tip of the iceberg. Look through other clip art sources to find inspiration and ideas for designs to use as patterns.

Now for the fun part! Because you have taken

the time to carefully prepare your design template for your particular piece of glass, etching will be quick and easy. This section describes the basic techniques of etching plus some etching strokes and tips.

Etching Techniques

1. Set up a work area. It is important to choose a location that has good ventilation and adequate light. A comfortable work table and chair are important. Gather materials and arrange them within reach.

2. Clean the glass to remove any labels, dirt or dust.

3. Place glass on a dark surface or cradle in a dark colored towel.

4. After reading the manufacturer's instructions and safety guidelines carefully, choose the appropriate bit called for in your project.

5. Begin etching by tracing the design with your tool just as you would trace with a pencil. Etch all dark areas and proceed slowly because all marks are permanent.

Note: The low to medium speeds work best for all projects. It is important to try to keep a steady hand while

etching. Make sure to hold the tool as close to the bit as possible without touching the rotating shaft, also keep the heel of your hand firmly on the table or glass piece and move the tool by pivoting your wrist. It is also helpful to use your free hand to steady the hand holding the tool.

6. Wash off any remaining ink marks with soap and water or glass cleaner.

7. Look over your design and touch up, fill in or smooth out edges as needed. The smallest diamond point bit works well for the finishing touches.

Etching Marks

Here are a few of the etching strokes that are used in some of our projects.

Strokes: This is especially useful when etching leaves. When etching large inside areas, use a series of strokes to form the solid area. This will give the foliage a more organic look.

Stippling: This easy technique is wonderful for creating texture. Using the smallest diamond point bit, just dot the glass as you would dot an "i." By etching several dots in a close vicinity, the illusion of shading will quickly emerge.

Circular Strokes: To create an oval shape as used in the fern leaf, touch the bit to the glass and slowly rotate the tool in a circular motion.

Etching tip: In this book, it is recommended when etching glass that will be used for food or beverage, to etch on the underside or outside of the glass object. This is so that the etched areas will not directly touch any food. It is not necessarily harmful for food to contact etched areas; it just makes cleaning your glass pieces a little easier.

Get the party started!

How would you like to add some spice to your Mexican fiesta, some sophistication to Martini night or have everyone raving about your one of a kind place cards? In this chapter we have chosen some fun and popular themes that will dazzle your guests. Entertaining has never been so much fun! Etched glass can add a personal and unique touch to any special event. From cocktail parties to romantic dinners for two under candle lit lanterns, our party ideas will set the tone for a variety of events.

Create a Mexican Fiesta!
Margarita Glasses and Vase

Mexican fiesta themed parties or dinners are perfect for summer entertaining. Spice up your festivities with some mouth-watering margaritas served up in hand-etched glasses. The star motif vase makes a colorful container filled with limes or arrange some fresh cut flowers in it for a centerpiece.

Etching time:
10 minutes per glass
30 minutes for the vase

Hint: when etching on any glass pieces that will be used for food, be sure to etch on the outside of the glass -not on the side that will have contact with food.

Supplies:

Margarita glasses, 4-1/2" dia. x 6-3/4" h
Vase - 4" w x 4" d x 7-3/4" h
Small and large diamond point bits
Masking tape
Permanent marker
Glass cleaner
Paper towels

Techniques:

Setting up Guidelines
Basic Technique for Transferring
Sizing and Tracing Repeat Borders
Etching Techniques

> Please read the Basic Techniques section before beginning your project.

Instructions:

1. Copy or trace the pattern. Resize to fit your glass if necessary.

2. For the glasses, set up guidelines on the top rim of the glass where the border will go.

3. Secure pattern inside the glass with tape.

4. Trace the patterns onto the glass using a black permanent marker.

5. Be sure to fill in all areas that you wish to etch with the marker (such as the triangle areas on the border). This will greatly reduce any confusion when you are etching.

6. Etch all marked areas using the large bit for big areas and the smaller bit for tight edges and corners. Use the circular etching motion in the "Etching Techniques" section for the dots in the pattern.

7. Clean off remaining marker with soap and water or glass cleaner.

8. Touch up as needed with the small bit.

9. Now, move onto the vase. Secure and trace the pattern inside the vase. Then etch. Enjoy your new glasses and vase! 🐇

Margarita vase pattern

Margarita glass pattern

Mini Vase Place Cards

An innovative twist on paper place cards.
These little vases are perfect for luncheons
or dinner parties and also serve as a
thoughtful party favor.

Etching time:
5 minutes per vase

Mini Vase Place Cards

Supplies:

Assorted mini glass vases, 2-1/2" dia. x 3"
Large and small diamond point bits
Masking tape or double-sided tape
Permanent marker
Glass cleaner
Paper towels
Ballpoint pen or stylus
Carbon paper

Techniques:

Tracing Type Fonts
Alternative Transferring Techniques:
      Using Carbon Paper
      Using the Computer

> Please read the Basic Techniques section before beginning your project.

Instructions:

1. Create patterns by tracing from the included type font pattern. Or you may choose to type names out on your computer in the font of your choice and print. Another option is to carefully write out the names freehand in permanent marker directly onto the vase using tape as a guide.

2. Place the pattern inside the vase and secure with tape.

3. If using a dark color of glass such as the cobalt blue, it will be difficult to see the pattern when placed inside the vase. Use one of the Alternative Transferring Techniques.

4. Carefully trace or write the names onto the surface of the glass using a permanent marker.

5. Carefully etch names using the largest diamond point bit. However, if a name is particularly long, you may opt for the smaller bit.

6. Clean off remaining ink with soap and water or glass cleaner.

7. Touch up if needed. ❧

Hint: Use double-sided tape to adhere pattern to small locations like these bud vases. It is less cumbersome than masking tape.

Aa Bb Cc Dd Ee

Ff Gg Hh Ii Jj Kk

Ll Mm Nn Oo Pp

Qq Rr Ss Tt Uu V

v Ww Xx Yy Zz

1234567890.!?

"$ *& +=!

Mini Vase Placecards alphabet

Etching time:
5 minutes per lantern

Four Season Party Lanterns

An Asian themed party is fun any time of year! These lanterns can serve as decorative tabletop enhancements or hang them from a tree branch to create a romantic setting. Winter, Spring, Summer or Fall, these lanterns create an inviting atmosphere anytime of year.

Supplies:

Round glass lanterns or vases, 3-1/2" dia. x 3-1/4" h (excludes handle)
Large diamond point bit
Masking tape
Permanent marker
Glass cleaner
Paper towels

Techniques:

Basic Technique for Transferring
Etching Techniques

Instructions:

1. Copy or trace the desired patterns. Resize to fit your lantern or vase if necessary.

2. Secure pattern to the inside of the piece and trace with a permanent marker. When tracing the pattern, remember to take time to fill in all areas to be etched.

3. Carefully etch all marked areas.

4. Clean off remaining ink with soap and water or glass cleaner.

5. Touch up edges as needed. ✍

> Please read the Basic Techniques section before beginning your project.

spring

summer

秋

fall

winter

Four Season Party Lantern Patterns

Hint: An alternate pattern for these lanterns is the Plum Blossom pattern. Just size it down and it will fit nicely into the Asian theme.

Cocktails!

Martini Glasses

The sophistication of a Martini matches perfectly with
these elegantly designed cocktail glasses. This pattern
is also beautiful on wine glasses and tumblers.

Supplies:

Martini glasses, 4-3/4" dia. x 8" h
Small diamond point bit
Permanent marker
Masking tape or double-sided tape
Ruler
Glass cleaner
Paper towels

Techniques:

Setting up Guidelines
Etching Techniques
Sizing and Transferring Repeat Borders

Please read the Basic Techniques section
before beginning your project.

Martini Glass pattern

Instructions:

1. Copy or trace the pattern. Resize to fit your glasses if
necessary.

2. Set up guidelines as explained in the Basic Techniques.
This will ensure that your pattern does not slant as you
trace around the glass.

3. Place the pattern inside the guidelines on the interior of
the glass. Secure with tape.

4. Trace the pattern with a permanent marker section by
section until it wraps completely around. When tracing
the pattern take time to fill in all areas to be etched.

5. Using the small diamond point bit, carefully etch all
marked areas.

6. Clean off remaining ink with soap and water or glass
cleaner.

7. Touch up as needed. ✍

Hint: Glasses with stems can be awkward to
hold while etching. Use a towel to cradle the glass
upside down.

Children's Birthday Party

Party Favors

Turn recycled glass soda bottles into personalized party favors for a child's birthday party. These bottles look adorable filled with fruit punch and also make a fun little gift for the well wishers.

Supplies:

Assorted recycled soda bottles

Large diamond point bits

Masking tape or double-sided tape

Permanent marker

Cardstock

Craft knife

Glass cleaner

Paper towels

Techniques:

Alternative Transferring Techniques

Using Stencils

Using Carbon Paper

Using the Computer

Etching Techniques

Instructions:

1. Copy or trace the pattern or select a type font of your choice.

2. Create a stencil using instructions from the "Basic Techniques - Using Stencils."

3. Trace the stencil with the permanent marker and fill in all areas to be etched.

4. Carefully etch all dark areas using the largest diamond point bit.

5. Clean off remaining ink with soap and water or glass cleaner.

6. Touch up if needed. ✦

Please read the Basic Techniques section before beginning your project.

Hints: Be sure to have extra glass bottles on hand in case a mistake is made.

AaBbCcDdEeFfGgHhIiJjKkLlMm
NnOoPpQqRrSsTtUuVvWwXxYyZz
1234567890. ! ? " * $ &+=':

Children's
Birthday
Party
alphabet

Accents for the Home

Every room needs a little decorative touch to add personality and interest. Etch an Italian inspired table top for a cozy outdoor patio, an elegant bordered bowl for a centerpiece or a fun set of juice glasses to start your morning. From beautiful to practical, on the following pages you will find a variety of glass accents for almost every room in your house!

Fern Vase
Elegant and Simple

This vase looks wonderful with a candle burning
inside or filled with fresh cut flowers.

Supplies:

Vase or hurricane shaped glass - 5-3/4" dia. x 9" h
Large and small diamond point bits
Permanent marker
Masking tape or double-sided tape
Glass cleaner
Paper towels

Techniques:

Basic Technique for Transferring
Etching Techniques: Circular Strokes

Please read the Basic Techniques section
before beginning your project.

Instructions:

1. Copy or trace the pattern. Resize to fit your vase if necessary.

2. Place pattern inside of the vase. Secure with tape.

3. Trace the pattern with a permanent marker, taking time to fill in all areas to be etched.

4. Using the small diamond point bit, carefully etch the spine of the fern leaf and the center spine of each individual branch.

5. Using the large diamond point bit, etch the leaves on the fern branches using a circular stroke motion.

6. Clean off remaining ink with soap and water or glass cleaner.

7. Touch up as needed. ✎

Hint: these vases look stunning as a pair.

Etching time:
25 minutes

Fern Vase

Fern Vase pattern

Kitchen Canisters

Americana designed containers for dry goods

Pull those old canisters out of the pantry and replace them with clearly labeled, personalized etched glass canisters.

Etching time:
10 minutes each

Supplies:

Glass canisters (with tight fitting lids):

    6" w x 6" d x 8" h   and

    5" w x 5" d x 6-3/4" h

Large and small diamond point bits

Permanent marker

Masking tape or double-sided tape

Ruler

Glass cleaner

Paper towels

Techniques:

Basic Technique for Transferring

Tracing Type Fonts

Etching Techniques: Circular Strokes

> Please read the Basic Techniques section before beginning your project.

Sugar Canister pattern

Instructions:

1. Copy or trace the pattern. Resize to fit your canisters if necessary.

2. Place pattern inside of the canister and use a ruler to insure a straight line. Secure with tape.

3. Trace the pattern with a permanent marker, taking time to fill in all areas to be etched.

4. Remove the pattern.

5. Use the circular stroke technique with the small or large diamond point bit. Carefully etch all marked areas.

6. Clean off remaining ink with soap and water or glass cleaner.

7. Touch up with small bit as needed. ☙

Salt Canister pattern

Flour Canister pattern

Etching time:
60-90 minutes

Italian Grotto Table

Glass Table Top

Inspired by a traditional Renaissance Italian pattern, this table makes any corner of your garden or patio cozy and inviting.

Supplies:

Round tempered glass top, 20" dia x 3/8" thick
Large diamond point bit
Permanent marker
Masking tape or double-sided tape
Ruler
Glass cleaner
Paper towels

Techniques:

Basic Technique for Transferring
Etching Techniques
Setting up Guidelines
Sizing and Transferring Repeat Borders

Please read the Basic Techniques section before beginning your project.

Instructions:

1. Copy or trace the pattern. Resize to fit your tabletop if necessary.

2. Draw guidelines 1" and 2" from the outside. You will have the 2 lines going all the way around the tabletop.

3. Position the pattern under the tabletop with the guidelines and secure with tape.

4. Be sure to fill in all areas that will be etched so as not to cause confusion during etching.

5. Trace the pattern with a permanent marker, taking time to fill in all areas to be etched.

6. Using the large diamond point bit, carefully etch all marked areas. Note- you can etch on the top or bottom of the glass table, whichever you prefer.

7. Clean off remaining ink with soap and water or glass cleaner.

8. Touch up as needed. ✑

Hints: This pattern is also stunning on square shapes. It is easy to adapt by using the guideline technique.

Italian Grotto Table pattern

Elegant Bottle Necked Vase

A recycled glass water bottle is transformed into a
stunning vase with a stylish plum blossom motif.

Supplies:

Recycled glass water bottle - 3-1/2" dia. x 12-1/2" h
Large and small diamond point bits
Masking tape or double-sided tape
Permanent marker
Glass cleaner
Paper towels
Carbon paper
Ball point pen or stylus

Techniques:

Alternative Transferring Techniques: Using Carbon Paper
Etching Techniques

Please read the Basic Techniques section
before beginning your project.

Instructions:

1. Copy or trace the pattern. Resize to fit your glass
bottle if necessary.

2. Position the pattern on the bottle and secure with
tape on two sides.

3. Place carbon paper between the pattern and the
bottle (transfer side toward the bottle) then trace the
pattern using a ball point pen or stylus. Remove pattern and carbon paper.

4. Retrace the pattern with a permanent marker, taking time to fill in all the areas to be etched.

5. Carefully etch all marked areas.

6. Clean off remaining ink with soap and water or
glass cleaner.

7. Touch up if needed. ☙

Hints: This vase makes a wonderful addition to
your home as well as a thoughtful gift for a friend.

Etching time:
20 minutes

Plum Blossom Bottle Pattern

Kitchen Window Herb Garden Pots

Basil, Rosemary, and Thyme.

This trio of herbs will brighten any
kitchen window sill and will also lend
a hand in the cooking department!

Rosemary

Sage

Basil

Kitchen Window Herb
Garden Patterns

Kitchen Window Herb Garden

Supplies:

Small glass flower pots, 2-3/4" dia. x 2-3/4" h

Small diamond point bit

Permanent marker

Masking tape or double-sided tape

Glass cleaner

Paper towels

Techniques:

Basic Technique for Transferring

Etching Techniques

> Please read the Basic Techniques section
> before beginning your project.

Instructions:

1. Copy or trace the pattern. Resize to fit your glass pots if necessary.

2. Place pattern inside of the pot and secure with tape.

3. Trace the pattern with a permanent marker, taking time to fill in all areas to be etched. Remove the pattern.

4. Carefully etch all marked areas.

5. Clean off remaining ink with soap and water or glass cleaner.

6. Touch up with small bit as needed. ✄

Hints: You can also use small, recycled glass jars for herb containers.

Rise and Shine!

Mornings will be bright with this retro
rooster pitcher and juice glasses.

Rise and Shine!

Supplies:

Glass pitcher

Juice glasses

Small and large diamond point bits

Permanent marker

Masking tape or double-sided tape

Glass cleaner

Paper towels

Techniques:

Basic Technique for Transferring

Etching Techniques: Stippling

Please read the Basic Techniques section before beginning your project.

Instructions:

1. Copy or trace the pattern. Resize to fit your pitcher or glasses if necessary.

2. Place pattern inside of the glass and secure with tape.

3. Trace the pattern with a permanent marker, taking time to fill in all areas to be etched. Remove the pattern.

4. Using the small diamond point bit, carefully etch all marked areas. Use the Stippling Technique for the bird feed.

5. Clean off remaining ink with soap and water or glass cleaner.

6. Touch up with small bit as needed. 🐦

Rise and Shine pattern

Etching time:
20 minutes per glass
35 minutes for pitcher

Acorn and Oak Leaf Bowl

An elegant border on a large bowl makes a wonderful centerpiece or focal point in a room.

Etching time:
60 minutes

Acorn and Oak Leaf Bowl Pattern

Acorn and Oak Leaf Bowl

Supplies:

Large glass bowl, 12" dia. x 7" h

Small and large diamond point bits

Permanent marker

Masking tape or double-sided tape

Glass cleaner

Paper towels

Techniques:

Sizing and Transferring Repeat Borders

Setting up Guidelines

Etching Techniques: Strokes

Please read the Basic Techniques section before beginning your project.

Instructions:

1. Copy or trace the pattern. Resize to fit your bowl if necessary.

2. With a permanent marker, draw guidelines around the outside rim of the bowl 3/4" and 1-3/4" from the top. This will ensure that your pattern does not slant as you trace around the glass.

3. Place the repeat pattern inside of the guidelines on the interior of the glass. Secure with tape.

4. Trace the pattern with permanent marker section by section until it wraps completely around. When tracing the pattern take time to fill in all areas to be etched.

5. Using the small diamond point bit, carefully etch all marked areas. When etching the oak leaves, use the stroke technique.

6. Clean off remaining ink with soap and water or glass cleaner.

7. Touch up as needed with small bit. ✎

Hint: Any of the border patterns included in this book would look stunning on a large glass bowl.

Bedside Water Carafe

This design was inspired by an
antique quilt and will certainly
brighten any bedroom.

Etching time:
20 minutes

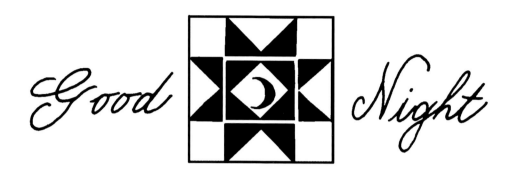

Bedside Water Carafe Pattern

Bedside Water Carafe

Supplies:

Glass carafe, 4-1/2" dia. x 7" h
Large and small diamond point bits
Masking tape or double-sided tape
Permanent marker
Glass cleaner
Paper towels
Carbon paper
Ball point pen or stylus

Techniques:

Alternative Transferring Techniques:
Using Carbon Paper
Using Stencils
Using Rubber Stamps
Etching Techniques
Tracing Type Fonts

Please read the Basic Techniques section before beginning your project.

Instructions:

1. Copy or trace the pattern. Resize to fit your glass carafe if necessary.

2. Position the pattern on the outside of the carafe and secure with tape on two sides.

3. Place carbon paper between the pattern and the glass with the carbon side toward the glass.

4. Trace the pattern with a ball point pen or stylus. Remove the pattern and carbon paper.

5. Retrace the pattern with a permanent marker, taking time to fill in all areas to be etched.

6. Using the large diamond point bit, etch all marked areas.

7. Clean off remaining ink with soap and water or glass cleaner.

8. Touch up with small diamond point if needed. ☞

Hints: This is a thoughtful addition to a guest bedroom.

Elegant Wine Decanter

The dark burgundy of red wine
sets off this grape leaf pattern exquisitely.

Etching time:
45 minutes

Elegant Wine Decanter

Supplies:

Glass wine decanter, 7" dia. x 9-1/4" h

Large and small diamond point bits

Masking tape or double-sided tape

Permanent marker

Glass cleaner

Paper towels

Carbon paper

Ballpoint pen or stylus

Please read the Basic Techniques section before beginning your project.

Techniques:

Alternative Transferring Techniques:

    Using Carbon Paper

    Setting up Guidelines

Etching Techniques:

    Strokes

Hint: It is a good idea to use guidelines, as explained in the Setting up Guidelines section to set the parameters for this design.

Instructions:

1. Copy or trace the pattern. Resize to fit your decanter if necessary.

2. Position the pattern on the outside of the carafe and secure with tape on two sides.

3. Place carbon paper between the pattern and the glass with the carbon side toward the glass.

4. Trace the pattern with a ball point pen or stylus. Remove the pattern and carbon paper.

5. Retrace the pattern with a permanent marker taking time to fill in all areas to be etched.

6. Using the large diamond point bit, etch all marked areas.

7. Clean off remaining ink with soap and water or glass cleaner.

8. Touch up with small diamond point if needed.

Elegant Wine Decanter Pattern. Enlarge 120% for actual size.

Holidays and Special Occasions

This special holiday section includes some wonderful and creative ways of adding a personal touch to your holiday celebrations. From a snowflake patterned plate full of cookies to a romantic twist on a valentine's bouquet of roses, you will surely feel the holiday spirit in these personalized gifts and accents for the home. The following pages provide ideas to help you brighten the holidays.

Snowflake Cookie Plate

This festive snowflake pattern
makes a wonderful hostess gift for all the
holiday parties you attend.

Supplies:

Large glass plate, 13" dia.
Small and large diamond point bits
Permanent marker
Masking tape or double-sided tape
Glass cleaner
Paper towels

Techniques:

Basic Technique for Transferring
Etching Techniques

Please read the Basic Techniques section before beginning your project.

Instructions:

1. Copy or trace the pattern. Resize to fit your glass plate if necessary.

2. You can draw the pattern on either side of the plate but be sure to etch on the underside of the plate so that etched areas will not have direct contact with food.

3. Secure pattern with tape.

4. Trace the pattern with a permanent marker, taking time to fill in all areas to be etched. Remove the pattern.

5. Using the large diamond point bit, carefully etch all marked areas. Use the small diamond point bit to etch tight edges and small details.

6. Clean off remaining ink with soap and water or glass cleaner.

7. Touch up with small bit as needed. ✺

Hint: The snowflake motif is wonderful on glass mugs, votives, vases and just about anything that you want to give a wintertime touch.

Etching time:
45 minutes

Snowflake Plate Patterns

Holiday Ornaments

Personalized with names and dates, these
Christmas ornaments make terrific keepsakes.

Etching time:
10 minutes each

Holiday Ornaments

Supplies:

Glass rounds with drilled holes and polished edges, 4" diameter

Small and large diamond point bits

Permanent marker

Masking tape or double-sided tape

Glass cleaner

Paper towels

Techniques:

Basic Technique for Transferring

Etching Techniques

> Please read the Basic Techniques section before beginning your project.

Instructions:

1. Have your local glass shop cut and polish these 4" rounds and drill a hole about 1/2" from the edge.

2. Copy or trace the pattern.

3. Place pattern underneath the glass and secure with tape. Double-sided tape works well here.

4. Trace the pattern with a permanent marker, taking time to fill in all areas to be etched. Remove the pattern.

5. Using the large diamond point bit, carefully etch all marked areas.

6. Use the small diamond point bit to etch tight edges and small details.

7. Clean off remaining ink with soap and water or glass cleaner.

8. Touch up with small bit as needed. ❧

Tips: This project is perfect for adding a personal touch. Names, dates and phrases can easily be added to any of these designs.

2004

Holiday Ornament Patterns

Holiday Goodies

Share some homemade preserves or freshly prepared salsa with friends and family over the holidays. Give your creations a logo or a fun name to add an extra special touch.

Etching time:
10 minutes each

Holiday Goodies

Lynn's homemade blueberry jelly

Tip: If you do not practice the art of canning food, purchase jars of preserves, sauces and condiments and personalize with etched fruits or the name of the gift receiver.

Maria's ✳ ✳ ✳ Salsa

Holiday Goodies Patterns

Supplies:

Homemade or store-bought preserves, 2-3/4" w x 2-3/4" d x 4" h

Large and small diamond point bits

Masking tape or double-sided tape

Permanent marker

Glass cleaner

Paper towels

Carbon paper

Ball point pen or stylus

Techniques:

Alternative Transferring Techniques:

Using Carbon Paper

Etching Techniques

> Please read the Basic Techniques section before beginning your project.

Instructions:

1. Copy or trace the pattern. Resize to fit your glass jar if necessary.

2. Position the pattern on the outside of the jar and secure with tape on two sides.

3. Place carbon paper between the pattern and the glass with the carbon side toward the glass.

4. Trace the pattern with a ball point pen or stylus. Remove the pattern and carbon paper.

5. Retrace the pattern with a permanent marker, taking time to fill in all areas to be etched.

6. Using the large diamond point bit, etch all marked areas.

7. Clean off remaining ink with soap and water or glass cleaner.

8. Touch up with small diamond point if needed. ✎

Hint: Etch jars for homemade goods before you do your canning.

AaBbCcDdEeFfGgHhIiJjKkLl
MmNnOoPpQqRrSsTtUuVvWwXxYyZz
1234567890 . !? " * $&+=':

Blueberry Preserves alphabet - small letters

AaBbCcDdEeFfGgHhIi
JjKkLlMmNnOoPp2qRrSs
TtUuVvWwXxYy3z
1234567890 . !? " * $&+=':

Blueberry Preserves alphabet - large letters

AaBbCcDdEeFfGgHhIi
JjKkLlMmNnOoPpQqRr
SsTtUuVvWwXxYyZz
1234567890 . !? " * $&+=':

Salsa alphabet

Valentine's Votives

A perfect gift for your Valentine. These votives
can be used as candles or bud vases. Place a single red rose in
each vase for a slight twist on the traditional bouquet.

Supplies:

Shot glasses, 2" dia. x 3-1/2"
Small and large diamond point bits
Masking tape or double-sided tape
Permanent marker
Glass cleaner
Paper towels
Ruler

Techniques:

Basic Technique for Transferring
Etching Techniques
Tracing Type Fonts

Instructions:

1. Copy or trace the pattern. If necessary, resize so that each letter will fit your glass.

2. Use a ruler to measure locations for each letter so that they will be consistent.

3. Place pattern inside of the glass and secure with tape.

4. Trace the pattern with a permanent marker, taking time to fill in all areas to be etched. Remove the pattern.

5. Using the large diamond point bit, carefully etch all marked areas.

6. Clean off remaining ink with soap and water or glass cleaner.

7. Touch up with small bit as needed.

8. Place candles or flowers in votives.

Tips: You can spell out anything your heart
desires! Write out a quick love note or a pet name
such as " be mine" or "cutie pie." It's easy to have
fun and personalize these glass votives.

Please read the Basic Techniques section
before beginning your project.

Etching time:
5 minutes each

A a B b C c D d

I i J j K k L l

P p Q q R r S s

X x Y y Z z

! ? " * $ & + = ' :

Valentine Votive alphabet

EeFfGgHh

MmNnOo

TtUuVvWw

1234567890 .

Memorable Gifts

Are you always looking for unique and special gifts for every occasion? The following pages have a large selection of gift ideas that are not only beautiful but heartfelt as well. Give a gift full of summer memories, personalize a vase with a monogram, or share your favorite bubble bath concoction with friends. Personalized etched glass makes a thoughtful gift for every occasion.

Brad in Vernazza, Italy, sitting on our favorite cliff. Watching the sunset and sipping some wine. June 2002.

Etching time:
10 minutes

Aa Bb Cc Dd Ee Ff Gg Hh Ii
Jj Kk Ll Mm Nn Oo Pp Qq R
r Ss Tt Uu Vv Ww Xx Yy Zz
1234567890 .!?" *$&+=':

Champagne
Bottle alphabet

Champagne Bottle

A perfect gift for a wedding or anniversary, this hand etched and personalized bottle marks a special occasion and makes a thoughtful and unique gift.

Supplies:

Champagne bottle
Large and small diamond point bits
Masking tape or double-sided tape
Permanent marker
Glass cleaner
Paper towels
Carbon paper
Ball point pen or stylus
Gold marking pen for glass (optional)

Techniques:

Alternative Transferring Techniques
    Using Carbon Paper
    Using Stencils
    Using Rubber Stamps
Setting Up Guidelines
Sizing and Transferring Repeat Borders
Etching Techniques

> Please read the Basic Techniques section before beginning your project.

Instructions:

1. Copy or trace the pattern. Resize to fit your bottle if necessary.

2. Position the pattern face up on the outside of the carafe and secure with tape on two sides.

3. Place carbon paper between the pattern and the glass with the carbon side toward the glass.

4. Trace the pattern with a ball point pen or stylus. Remove the pattern and carbon paper.

5. Retrace the pattern with a permanent marker, taking time to fill in all areas to be etched.

6. Using the large diamond point bit, etch all marked areas.

7. Clean off remaining ink with soap and water or glass cleaner.

8. Touch up with small diamond point if needed.

9. For added elegance, fill the etched areas with a gold marker designed to work on glass. Allow it to dry for a minute or two, and then wipe any excess gold ink from around the etched area with a damp paper towel. Take care not to remove the ink on the etched areas. ✍

Hint: Write names, dates or even a poem to make this truly a special gift.

Champagne Glasses and Ice Bucket

Monograms are a traditional way to personalize
glass. This monogram with a garland border makes a
wonderful gift for special occasions.

Supplies:

Ice bucket, 7-3/4" dia. x 8-3/4" h
Champagne glasses, 2" dia. x 8-3/4" h
Small and large diamond point bits
Permanent marker
Masking tape or double-sided tape
Glass cleaner
Paper towels

Techniques:

Basic Technique for Transferring
Setting Up Guidelines
Sizing and Transferring Repeat Borders
Tracing Type Fonts
Etching Techniques

Please read the Basic Techniques section
before beginning your project.

Instructions:

1. Copy or trace the pattern. Resize to fit your ice bucket
or glasses if necessary.

2. For the glasses: place pattern inside of the glass and
secure with tape.

3. Trace the pattern with a permanent marker, taking time
to fill in all areas to be etched. Remove the pattern.

4. Using the small diamond point bit, carefully etch all
marked areas.

5. For the ice bucket: place the template inside the glass
bucket. Trace the pattern with a permanent marker, taking
time to fill in all areas to be etched. Remove the pattern
and etch using the small diamond point bit.

6. Clean off remaining ink with soap and water or glass
cleaner.

7. Touch up with small bit as needed. ✎

Tips: For a more formal monogram, choose a
script type font from our pattern selection.

Etching time:
15 minutes per glass
25 minutes for ice bucket

AABBCcD

HHIIJJ

NNOOPP

TTUUVV

YYZZ

Champagne Glasses and Ice Bucket alphabet and pattern
Note: Use large letters for bucket and small letters for glasses

Dᴅ Eᴇ Fғ Gɢ

Kᴋ Lʟ Mᴍ

Qǫ Rʀ Ss

Wᴡ Xx

Monogrammed Vase

Personal and classic, monograms add a special touch
to a plain glass vase. This elegant monogram makes a
beautiful and personalized gift. Here we have used an
ornate, art deco styled letter "T".

Etching time:
45 minutes

Monogrammed Vase

Supplies:

Glass vase, 6-1/2" dia. x 10-1/2" h
Large and small diamond point bits
Masking tape or double-sided tape
Permanent marker
Glass cleaner
Paper towels

Techniques:

Basic Technique for Transferring
Etching Techniques
Tracing Type Fonts

Please read the Basic Techniques section
before beginning your project.

Instructions:

1. Copy or trace pattern. Resize to fit your vase if necessary.

2. Place pattern inside of the glass and secure with tape.

3. Trace the pattern with a permanent marker, taking time to fill in all areas to be etched. Remove the pattern.

4. Using the large diamond point bit, carefully etch all marked areas. Clean off remaining ink with soap and water or glass cleaner.

5. Touch up with small bit as needed.

Tips: For this project we recycled a vase that came with a flower arrangement from the florist. For other monogrammed letters, browse through our font patterns and search craft stores for clip art, stencils or stamps.

Etching time:
30 minutes

Monogrammed Vase Pattern

Olive Branch Salad Plates

A set of four of these plates makes a fabulous shower, wedding, or any occasion gift!

Olive Branch Salad Plate Pattern

Olive Branch Salad Plates

Supplies:

Glass salad plates, 8" dia.
Small and large diamond point bits
Permanent marker
Masking tape or double-sided tape
Glass cleaner
Paper towels

Techniques:

Setting up Guidelines
Sizing and Transferring Repeat Borders
Basic Techniques for Transferring
Etching Techniques

> Please read the Basic Techniques section before beginning your project.

Instructions:

1. Copy or trace the pattern. Resize to fit your plate if necessary.

2. With a permanent marker, draw guidelines around the rim of the plate 3/8" and 1-3/4" from the top. This will ensure that your pattern does not slant as you go around the glass. You can draw the pattern on either side of the plate but be sure to etch on the underside of the plate so that etched areas will not have direct contact with food.

3. Secure pattern with tape.

4. Trace the pattern with a permanent marker, taking time to fill in all areas to be etched. Remove the pattern.

5. Using the large diamond point bit, carefully etch all marked areas. Use the small diamond point bit to etch tight edges and small details.

6. Clean off remaining ink with soap and water or glass cleaner.

7. Touch up with small bit as needed. ☜

Olive Branch repeat pattern

Tip: This design also looks great on a large plate to use as a serving piece or a party appetizer plate. Follow the instructions for Setting up Guidelines and Sizing and Tracing Repeat Borders.

Etching time:
45 minutes per plate

Etching time:
10 minutes

Beach Treasures Vase

This is a beautiful way to display summer's
seashells as well as a thoughtful gift for anyone
who enjoys the beach.

beach
treasures

Beach Treasures Vase Pattern

Beach Treasures Vase

Supplies:

Square glass vase, 6" w x 6" d x 6" h
Large and small diamond point bits
Masking tape or double-sided tape
Permanent marker
Glass cleaner
Paper towels
Sea shells

Techniques:

Basic Techniques for Transferring
Etching Techniques
Tracing Type Fonts

Please read the Basic Techniques section
before beginning your project.

Instructions:

1. Copy or trace the pattern. Resize to fit your vase if necessary.

2. Place pattern inside of the glass and secure with tape.

3. Trace the pattern with a permanent marker, taking time to fill in all areas to be etched. Remove the pattern.

4. Using the large diamond point bit, carefully etch all marked areas.

5. Clean off remaining ink with soap and water or glass cleaner.

6. Touch up with small bit as needed.

7. Fill with collected seashells. 🐚

Tip: No need to wrap up this gift, just tie a ribbon around the vase, attach a card and you will have a beautiful presentation for a gift full of summer memories.

Personalized Picture Frames

This is a perfect way to capture a memory. Best of all, you can record names, dates, and phrases in a decorative manner to accompany your photo.

Etching time:
15 minutes

Personalized Picture Frames

AaBbCcDdEeFfGgHhIiJj

KkLlMmNnOoPp2qRrSs

TtUuVvWwXxYy3z

1234567890 .!?"*$&+='∶

Picture Frame alphabet

Supplies:

Frame with glass pane, 5-1/2" w x 7-1/2" h
Small and large diamond point bits
Permanent marker
Masking tape or double-sided tape
Glass cleaner
Paper towels

Techniques:

Setting up Guidelines
Tracing Type Fonts
Basic Techniques for Transferring
Etching Techniques
Sizing and Transferring Repeat Borders

Please read the Basic Techniques section before beginning your project.

Instructions:

1. Determine where you wish to etch. Draw guidelines for the area to be etched. Be sure that the etched areas will not interfere with the picture inside the frame.

2. Copy or trace the type font. Resize to fit glass pane if necessary.

3. Place pattern underneath the glass and secure with tape.

4. Trace the pattern with a permanent marker, taking time to fill in all areas to be etched. Remove the pattern.

5. Using the large or small diamond point bit, carefully etch all marked areas.

6. Use the small diamond point bit to etch tight edges and small details.

7. Clean off remaining ink with soap and water or glass cleaner.

8. Touch up with small bit as needed. ✐

Tips: We have used fonts in this project, but you can also etch a decorative border or incorporate a monogram.

AaBbCcDdEeFfGgHhIiJj
KkLlMmNnOoPpQqRrSs
TtUuVvWwXxYyZz
1234567890 .!?"*$&+='∶

Optional type font for Picture Frame alphabet

AaBbCcDdEeFfGgHhIiJj
KkLlMmNnOoPpQqRrSs
TtUuVvWwXxYyZz
1234567890 .!?"*$&+=':

Optional type font for Picture Frame alphabet

Monogrammed Votive

This masculine design makes a wonderful gift. We have
used votives already filled with candles, but you can
also use juice glasses and place a candle inside.

Supplies:

Glass votives with candle, 2-1/4" dia. x 4" h
Large and small diamond point bits
Masking tape or double-sided tape
Permanent marker
Glass cleaner
Paper towels
Carbon paper or
Cardstock
Craft knife
Ballpoint pen or stylus

Techniques:

Alternative Tracing Techniques
Setting up Guidelines
Basic Techniques for Transferring
Etching Techniques
Tracing Type Fonts

> Please read the Basic Techniques section
> before beginning your project.

Tips: Because the shape of this votive mimics a
drinking glass, once the candle has expired, the glass
can be cleaned out and used for cocktails!

Instructions:

1. Copy or trace pattern. Resize to fit your votive or glass
if necessary.

2. The technique to use for transferring the pattern
depends on the glass you choose. If using a votive with an
opaque surface (because it has a candle affixed for example), you will need to use one of the Alternative Tracing
Techniques, such as Carbon Paper.

3. Position the pattern on the outside of the votive and
secure with tape on two sides.

4. Place carbon paper between the pattern and the glass
with the carbon side toward the glass.

5. Trace the pattern with a ball point pen or stylus.
Remove the pattern and carbon paper.

6. Retrace the pattern with a permanent marker, taking
time to fill in all areas to be etched.

7. Using the large or small diamond point bit, etch all
marked areas. Use the circular motion for etching the
leaves.

8. Clean off remaining ink with soap and water or glass
cleaner.

9. Touch up with small diamond point if needed. ✍

ABCD

JKLM

RSTUV

Monogrammed Votive alphabet

EFGHI

NOPQ

WXYZ

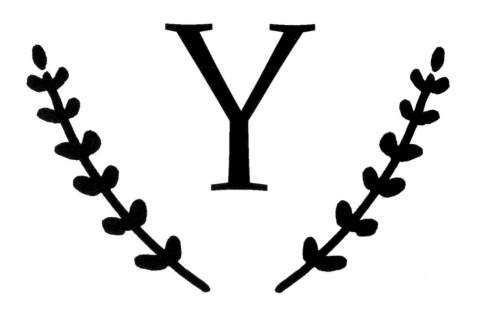

Monogrammed Votive pattern

Glass Coaster pattern (see page 105)

Glass Coasters

These fun, whimsical coasters make
a wonderful housewarming gift.

Etching time:
15 minutes per coaster

Glass Coasters

Supplies:

Glass squares with polished edges, 4" x 4" x 1/4" thick
Small and large diamond point bits
Permanent marker
Masking tape or double-sided tape
Glass cleaner
Paper towel
Ruler
Spray adhesive
Backing material such as art paper, construction paper, cork board, felt, or fabric
Craft knife

Techniques:

Basic Techniques for Transferring
Etching Techniques

Please read the Basic Techniques section before beginning your project.

Tips: When cutting the backing material, it is better to err on the larger size. This way you do not have to line up the edges perfectly, you can trim the edges once the paper has been glued to the glass.

Instructions:

1. Have your local glass shop cut and polish the edges of these 4" square glass shapes.

2. Copy or trace pattern.

3. Place pattern underneath the glass and secure with tape. Double-sided tape works well here.

4. Trace the pattern with a permanent marker, taking time to fill in all areas to be etched. Remove the pattern.

5. Using the large diamond point bit, carefully etch all marked areas.

6. Use the small diamond point bit to etch thin lines.

7. Clean off remaining ink with soap and water or glass cleaner.

8. Touch up with a small bit as needed.

9. Place the finished glass square on top of the desired paper or backing material.

10. Press down on the glass and lightly trace the edges with a pencil. Remove glass.

11. Use the ruler to measure about 1/4" border around the pencil drawn edge.

12. Place a cutting mat or cardboard underneath the backing material. This is important so that the table surface you are working on will not get cut with the knife. Cut the outside line with a craft knife.

13. Erase any remaining pencil lines.

14. Place the backing material on newspaper. Apply adhesive spray on one side of each piece of backing material. Do not use adhesive spray inside your home; it will coat surroundings and is very difficult to remove.

15. Place glue side onto the smooth side of the glass.

16. Trim excess material from edges with a craft knife.

Bath Accessories

Gifts for the bath are indulgent and luxurious. Create your own
line of bath amenities to decorate your bathroom or give them
as gifts - your friends will surely feel pampered!

Etching time:
20 minutes per bottle

Amy's
· bubble · bath ·

Melissa's
· · · · · · · · · ·
bath
oil

Relax
· · · · · · · · · ·
bath gel

Bath Accessories Patterns

Bath Accessories

Supplies:

Glass bottles with lids
    2-1/2" dia. x 5-1/4" h
Large and small diamond point bits
Masking tape or double-sided tape
Permanent marker
Glass cleaner
Paper towels
Carbon paper
Cardstock
Craft knife
Ball point pen or stylus

Techniques:

Alternative Transferring Techniques:
    Using Carbon Paper
Basic Techniques for Tracing
Etching Techniques
Tracing Type Fonts

> Please read the Basic Techniques section before beginning your project.

Instructions:

1. Copy or trace the pattern. Resize to fit your bottle if necessary.

2. Draw a straight line with a ruler and a permanent marker directly onto the glass, this serves as a guide.

3. There are two transferring techniques that would work well here. You can use the carbon paper or the stencil techniques as described in the alternative transferring section.

4. Position the pattern on the outside of the bottle and secure with tape on two sides.

5. For the carbon paper technique: Place carbon paper between the pattern and the glass with the carbon side toward the glass.

6. Trace the pattern with a ball point pen or stylus. Remove the pattern and carbon paper.

7. Retrace the pattern with a permanent marker, taking time to fill in all areas to be etched.

8. Using the large diamond point bit, etch all marked areas.

9. Clean off remaining ink with soap and water or glass cleaner.

10. Touch up with small diamond point if needed. ✇

Hints: corks and seashells make fun stoppers for these bottles.

Just for Kids, and pets too!

Welcome to the fun and whimsical side of glass etching! In this special section, you will find some innovative projects with children and pets in mind. From organizing and setting goals to embellishing dog and fish bowls, the following pages hold some playful and practical ideas.

Etching time:
10 minutes per jar

Toy Jars

What child doesn't love a personalized
gift made just for them! This is a fun
and innovative way to organize
and store children's toys.

Supplies:

Recycled glass jars: 6" dia. x 10" h and
4" dia. x 5-1/2" h, and 3" dia. x 5" h
Large and small diamond point bits
Permanent marker
Masking tape or double-sided tape
Ruler
Glass cleaner
Paper towels

Techniques:

Basic Techniques for Transferring
Etching Techniques
Tracing Type Fonts

> Please read the Basic Techniques section
> before beginning your project.

Instructions:

1. Copy or trace the pattern. Resize to fit your jar if necessary.

2. Draw a straight line with a ruler and permanent marker directly onto the glass. This serves as a guide.

3. Place pattern inside of the jar and position on the straight line. Secure with tape.

4. Trace the pattern with a permanent marker, taking time to fill in all areas to be etched. Remove the pattern.

5. Using the small or large diamond point bit, carefully etch all marked areas. Use the circular etching method for the decorative dots.

6. Clean off remaining ink with soap and water or glass cleaner.

7. Touch up with small bit as needed. ᕬ

Hint: check the recycle bin for different shapes and sizes of jars. Large pickle jars and recycled condiment containers work especially well for this project.

AaBbCcDdEeFfGg
HhIiJjKkLlMmNn
OoPpQqRrSsTt
UuVvWwXxYyZz
1234567890
.!?"*$&+='':

Toy Jars Alphabets
(3 sizes)

AaBbCcDdEeFfGgHhIi
JjKkLlMmNnOoPpQq
RrSsTtUuVvWwXxYyZz
1234567890
.!?"*$&+='':

AaBbCcDdEeFfGgHhIiJj
KkLlMmNnOoPpQqRrSs
TtUuVvWwXxYyZz
1234567890
.!?"*$&+='':

Piggy Bank

Piggy banks are wonderful aides for teaching
children the value of a dollar and setting
goals. With this design, it also makes saving
loose change a lot of fun.

Supplies:

Large glass jar, 6" dia. x 10" h
Large and small diamond point bits
Permanent marker
Masking tape or double-sided tape
Ruler
Glass cleaner
Paper towels

Techniques:

Basic Techniques for Transferring
Etching Techniques
Tracing Type Fonts

Please read the Basic Techniques section before beginning your project.

Instructions:

1. Copy or trace the pattern. Resize to fit your jar if necessary.

2. Draw a straight line with a ruler and permanent marker directly onto the glass. This serves as a guide.

3. Place pattern inside of the jar and position on the straight line. Secure with tape.

4. Trace the pattern with a permanent marker, taking time to fill in all areas to be etched. Remove the pattern.

5. Using the small or large diamond point bit, carefully etch all marked areas.

6. Clean off remaining ink with soap and water or glass cleaner.

7. Touch up with small bit as needed. ✎

Tips: Customize this project by adding names, phrases or other goals such as "savings for a rainy day", "my computer", "video games", "college tuition", "toy fund", etc…

Etching time:
20 minutes

my bike

Piggy Bank pattern

good

dog

Dog Treat Jar pattern

Dog Bowl pattern

Hint: you can cut a slot in the metal lid with your rotary tool and the appropriate bit. Check with the manufacturer or retailer for the right bit for the job.

Dog Treat Jar
and Food Bowls

All dog owners would agree that their pup is part of the family.
Every dog deserves a personalized place setting.

Etching time:
20 minutes per item

AaBbCcDdE

eFfGgHhIiJj

KkLlMmNn

OoPpQqRr

SsTtUuVv

WwXxYyZz

Dog Bowl alphabet

Etching time:
20 minutes per item

Fish Bowl

Although it is fun to collect and add aquarium gadgets for your
fish bowl, why not etch some fun illustrations on the outside glass.
These designs make a fresh and decorative alternative.

Supplies:

Fish bowl
Large and small diamond point bits
Permanent marker
Masking tape or double-sided tape
Glass cleaner
Paper towels

Techniques:

Basic Techniques for Transferring
Etching Techniques

> Please read the Basic Techniques section
> before beginning your project.

Instructions:

1. Copy or trace the pattern. Resize it to fit your fish bowl if necessary.

2. It is best to work this design in sections. First determine where you wish to place the designs. Our project has coral designs on 4 equally spaced locations in a north, south, east, west configuration. Next, decide where you would like the fish and starfish to appear. We have chosen to place them in between two coral patterns.

3. Draw 4 equally spaced tick marks with your marker on the top rim of the fishbowl. This will serve as a guide for the center of your coral pattern.

4. Place coral pattern inside of the fishbowl and center it using the tick marks on the top rim.

5. Secure with tape.

6. Trace the pattern with a permanent marker, first the outline of the coral and then randomly add dots.

7. Remove the pattern and repeat the tracing in the other three coral locations.

8. Place the fish and starfish patterns in between 2 coral branches. Trace with a permanent marker, taking time to fill in all areas to be etched. Remove pattern.

9. Using the small or large diamond point bit, start by etching the outline of the coral.

10. To etch the texture of dots use the Stippling technique. These are quick and easy to do. It is not necessary to follow the pattern to the dot, you can randomly place the dots throughout the inside of the coral.

11. Etch the fish using the large bit in the thicker areas, save the tight lines, like the fins, for the small bit.

12. Clean off remaining ink with soap and water or glass cleaner.

13. Touch up with small bit as needed. ☞

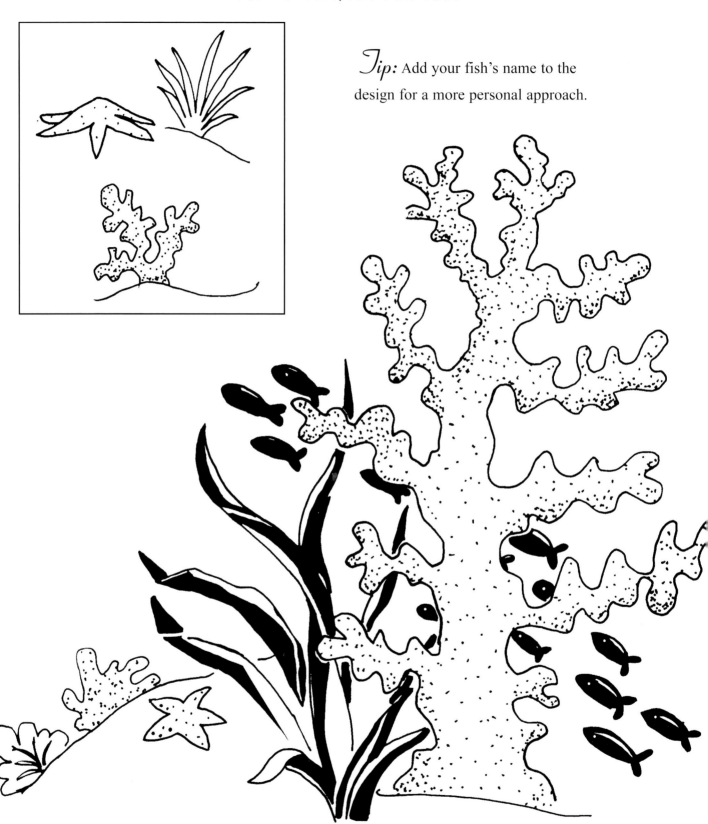

Tip: Add your fish's name to the design for a more personal approach.

Fish Bowl pattern

METRIC CONVERSION CHART

Inches to Millimeters and Centimeters

Inches	MM	CM
1/8	3	.3
1/4	6	.6
3/8	10	1.0
1/2	13	1.3
5/8	16	1.6
3/4	19	1.9
7/8	22	2.2
1	25	2.5
1-1/4	32	3.2
1-1/2	38	3.8
1-3/4	44	4.4
2	51	5.1
3	76	7.6
4	102	10.2
5	127	12.7
6	152	15.2
7	178	17.8
8	203	20.3
9	229	22.9
10	254	25.4
11	279	27.9
12	305	30.5

Yards to Meters

Yards	Meters
1/8	.11
1/4	.23
3/8	.34
1/2	.46
5/8	.57
3/4	.69
7/8	.80
1	.91
2	1.83
3	2.74
4	3.66
5	4.57
6	5.49
7	6.40
8	7.32
9	8.23
10	9.14

Index

INDEX

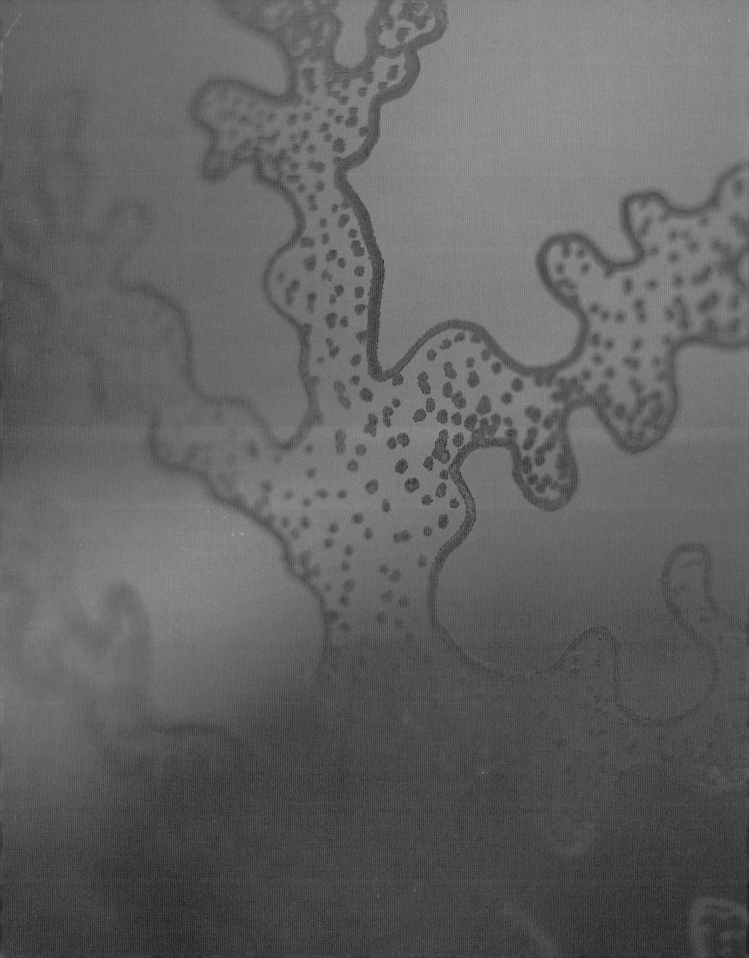